FRACTALS

Monique Liston

Presentation by *BookLeaf Publishing*

Web: www.bookleafpub.com

E-mail: info@bookleafpub.com

ISBN: 9789363319981

First edition 2024

This book is dedicated to you in the future, me in the past, and all of us right here and right now.

ACKNOWLEDGEMENT

I am not a poet.
I am barely a writer.
But I am most definitely committed to healing work, and poetry is healing work.

This collection of poems is only possible because I am loved so deeply by so many people across time and space.

I am prayed for.

This collection represents a snapshot in time when I had enough self-awareness to reflect and put things down on paper.

My gratitude goes to being relentlessly inspired by ancestors bell hooks, Toni Morrison, James Baldwin, John Henrik Clarke, Amos Wilson, Kwame Ture and many others.

I also am seen, in the most culturally relevant sense, by big-hearted thinkers in this world like Hess, Dominique, Matthew, Tyanna, Shavonda, Symphony, Venice, Radaya, and everyone who has ever been a part of that little project I call UBUNTU Research and Evaluation.

I have amazing friends and amazing family.

Lastly, to the future generations of Black women, femmes, and girls, may these words serve as a reminder of your potential and the infinite possibilities that lie ahead. You are the embodiment of freedom, the living dreams of our ancestors, and the architects of a liberated future.

PREFACE

Poetics are a tool for speaking to the existence of the inner life of Black individuals, offering a space to express emotions, thoughts, and experiences often erased, marginalized or suppressed in dominant (white) narratives. As Kevin Quashie suggests in *Black Aliveness and the Poetics of Being*, this articulation becomes a form of resistance, asserting the humanity and complexity of Black people by reclaiming the right to be fully seen and heard beyond the limitations imposed by oppressive structures. Poetry, in this sense, shapes and reshapes identity, challenging the erasure and invisibility often projected onto Black bodies and minds.

Beyond merely reflecting current realities, poetry is a powerful mechanism for imagining new possibilities and futures. adrienne maree brown, in *Emergent Strategy*, emphasizes that poetry is a medium for radical dreaming—allowing us to envision just, equitable, and liberated futures that transcend the physical and psychological constraints of the present. Through the act of poetic creation, individuals and communities are able to summon futures grounded in care, transformation, and freedom.

Edouard Glissant, in *Poetics of Relation*, furthers this notion by highlighting poetry's capacity to articulate the complex, intertwined relationships that define human existence. Poetry has the unique ability to explore and express the web of connections between people, environments, histories, and cultures, fostering a deep sense of relationality and collective belonging. It serves as both a mirror of the self and a bridge to the collective, enabling shared understanding across difference.

Poetry, then, is not just a tool for personal empowerment but also a collective one. The legacy of poets like Audre Lorde underscores this, as her work consistently demonstrated that poetry is not a luxury—it is a vital necessity for survival. Lorde's poetry, rooted in the assertion of Black womanhood and queerness, serves as an instrument of healing and revolution. Through its power to both disrupt and reimagine, poetics becomes a radical pathway to transformation, empowering both the individual and the community.

This series of poems reflects my framework for dignity.

Dignity represents the mutual acknowledgment
of self-worth between an individual and society.
Each person must recognize their inherent
worth, which is reflected in the value of those
around them. There are two core domains:
Aliveness and Accountability. The Dignity of
Aliveness, which affirms the inherent worth and
vibrant existence of Black human life beyond
the constraints of anti-Black sociopolitical
violence through autonomy, humanity, and
mutual rank and The Dignity of Accountability
ensures that these aspects, particularly the
Dignity of Aliveness, are both observable and
measurable in real-world experiences.

Through this collection's poems, you will
witness a dignified Black existence. Each poem
is an invocation, a spellcast toward liberation,
resonating with the dignity and resilience of
Black life. As you read, may you feel the echoes
of the past, the vibrations of the present, and the
aspirations for the future. May these words
inspire you to engage with the world more
deeply, to listen and inscribe your own truths,
and to speak to after with courage and
conviction.

In solidarity,
monique

BEGINNING OF A LOVE STORY

The beginning of this love story
is humiliation

                    The act of dignity denied

In a windowless room
In a nondescript building
On a campus

                    I feel no connection to

There is no fanfare
No D I R E C T hostility

                    I am alone

The terms and conditions
culturally bred in my bloodline for centuries
refused
Have you ever been struck with multiple
crushing blows to the chest
and have no witnesses?
No one here to testify
on Y O U R behalf
                This is attempted murder
                                my soul screamed.
attempted
but failed
The point of this so-called exercise
is to defend what I have produced
instead
instead
instead
                        I am asked O N E question
and when I respond
no one looks at me
listening seems more like a task than a
responsibility for them
I am asked to sit outside the windowless room
at the end of the narrow hallway
in an uncomfortable chair
I am not anxious
I am not eager
I am just
THERE

maybe no different than a book on the shelf
or, more likely,
no different than the discarded junk mail in the
trashcan
You know
         I don't even remember
          what I wore that day

me.
Black
and woman
on this day
With no recollection of my outfit
If you know
then you really know
The waiting is over
they call me back
Congratulations
      D O C T O R
I waited for some feelings or emotions to emerge
they didn't
the damage from those repeated blows to the
chest—
              done

I exit
alone
And the beginning of this love story
is
     humiliation

(RE)MEMBER US

langston hughes once said
                "my motto
            as I live and learn
                is to dig
             and be dug
              in return"

my mama said
remember langston
she had us read his poems
memorize stanzas
                    know
                     his
                    work

I don't forget him
I return to his words often
when I have questions
I see
is there anything
that connects
that might lead me
to new insights

it's not just him
because my professor told me
remember baldwin
and my homegirls told me
remember toni
and then I grew new friends
and they told me
remember audre
remember octavia
remember bell
remember marsha
and elders reminded me
remember john
remember asa
remember kwame
and of course

I remember Malcolm
so
hard

that I
cannot know
another

Oh yes
I remember now
fannie
harriet
amy jacques
nannie
hatsheptsut
 might as well have them tattooed under my right
breast

the dignified life
it seems
to me
is one
where you are seen as worthy

enough

to teach the next generations
to remember
you

FOUND POEM #1

a
second sight
into
Black futures
sees
language
and understands
the power of words
so consider
"Black life
is a science fiction experience,"
he said
"hm of course,"
I said
because
when

        you are local
            (to Black imaginations)
      you are accountable
            (to Black futures)

DIGNITY OF
RECOGNITION

i am so grateful
to have the chance
to bear witness to

quotidian

ubiquitous

Black love
over a table
of
steamed crabs
outside an RV
in southern Maryland

COPYCAT ON A GOOD DAY

they say that mimicry is the sincerest form of
flattery
        easy to say that
          when
you are being mimicked in a space of shared
belonging, protected dignity, and relational
balance
        But I am Black.
AND
There is no space of race neutrality
so race challenges the sincerity of mimicry
the resulting feeling is much more dire than
mere flattery
Whiteness
in order to sustain itself
as the

s
 u
  c
   c
    u
     b
      u
       s
it truly is
mimics
           the aesthetics of Blackness
and
through this poorly executed practice
the beauty of Blackness is ignored
swag and cool are easily observed,
photographed, and catalogued
but then consumed without history, memory,
spirituality, and study
o   v   e   r   generations
Whiteness
and White culture
are defined
           because what else is whiteness
        besides the practice of violent theft and
                    exploitation
reported back as
flattery.

AVERAGE WHITE GUY

average white guy said that the organization
needs to do an antiracism workshop

                                   I said, "oh."
average white guy went on to say that they are
average

                 I said, "what do you mean by that"
average white guy said that they are steeped in
systemic racism
*(I call him a v e r a g e white guy on purpose,
friend)*

I then asked, "what does that look like?"
average white guy says that white progressives
have a theoretical understanding but fail to
create better behavior
they cower as a system to the white dominant
group
they aren't committed to antiracism
and theory-based understanding does not always
translate into practice

I said, "well..."
average white guy continued to talk about the
white struggle in his organization
I continued to nod and express my PhD-awarded
          "hmms" and "uh-huhs" appropriately
average white guy talked to me for an hour
eventually
I said
    "Here's what I can do and here's what it would
                                           cost..."
I
never heard
from average white guy
again.

FROM KAREN (ANNOTATED)

I hope you will not take offense
(I already am, Karen)
but I felt you were dressed very inappropriately
in the photo,
(so?)
wearing a skin-tight white top
(it wasn't)
with your large breasts bulging out
(they weren't but obviously you were distracted)
and the skin-tight white top extending over your
stomach with a fair amount of weight. (I knew I
was fat when I woke up that day)

Is this a good role model for women of color?
(absolutely yes)
Is it professional looking and does it present an
image for aspiring black women?
(fuck yes)
Could you have selected a more appropriate
outfit for a publicity photo?
(unfortunately no)
There used to be a book called, *Dress for
Success*.
(it's outdated and harmful)
Gone are these days
(thank god)
but still there is some importance for a leader
(eyeball roll emoji)
especially a leader of color
(yes—this is a white woman)
to exhibit professional business attire, casual or
not.
(this doesn't even make sense)
I do see woman of color often dressing
suggestively with low cut cleavage exhibited.
(what does this have to do with me)
In showbusiness it may be the norm but in
public discretion would best serve your
community.
(reader, if you saw the shirt, you would be
disappointed)

JULY 13, 2024

how come
Black people
attract bullets
and the white supremacist
narrowly escapes them?

ANCESTRAL MEMORY
AND REVERENCE

I choose. You choose. We choose.
I be. You be. We be.
I go. You go. We go.
I do. You do. We do.
I am. You are. We are.
alive.
dignified.

JAMES, BELL, AND HESS

what torments me most
connects me with being alive

whose are you
who were they
who will you become
who did they become

because
they lit here—
in you and in me
and over there
in them and in you
the fire next time

CHRISTINA

it takes no psychic powers
to predict Black death
because the weather report will always say the
same thing
Partly Human
with a chance of Severe Heartbreak
nothing about Black death is a metaphor
it's everyday
it's the national anthem and currency of the
place I call home
Black death
a legacy of never actually addressing the evil in
the world
instead making room for comfort over humanity
access denied

access denied
access denied
didn't we send a prayer up about us?
it's like the receiver just keeps hitting
delete
delete
delete
and yet because it's Black dirt on a white world
to you
when we know it's an annoying dent in Black
aliveness for us
we die
we die
we die
in order to be
alive
alive
alive

DOMINIQUE

remember
we have to give reverence
for the living

                                          we belong

                                   we are visible

                                     we alive

nigga!

you hear me?

simply put sis

if you hand a girl a cocktail;
      hand a girl a bottle of water TOO!

PRESCRIPTION

the diagnosis is:
black girl alive and young
the treatment
only your sister can provide
dance girl
let's hold a cipher
i wanna write—
how do I feel about today?
how do I want the world to remember me?
dear sister
this is what I wish for you
do repeatedly
as often as possibly
until you are
still black
more girl
very alive
yet
not
as
young

THE HUMBLE POSITION

she said
"If I were one of the data points
in the story I am telling,
would I be offended?"
baby, then
you move yourself into that position
and make sure
not to offend yourself
and if you do—
'cuz you might—
be okay
and grateful
if anyone pays enough mind
to tell you

MAMA, WOLE and TCB

to speak
is to assume
a culture
and bear responsibility
for
a
nation
so what are you pretending not to know today,
sweetheart
when you were taught
to be confident
honest
and Black
so that you
as a spiritual being
can continue to breathe life
into
a
Black
world

I SEE YOU

when a Black man
dresses like Bill Murray
from
> *The Life Aquatic with*
> *Steve Zissou*

I am grateful for him

> using Wes Anderson

to give me
a visual treat

> that affirms my wild imagination

of him
living
happy

> dignified

> and free

HIT SAVE

Stop trusting the cloud
to remember
your joy
your struggle
your love
your memory
take the time
to
HIT SAVE

AI (ANNOTATED)

Please transform my headshot (WHY?)
into an anime character. (COLOR ME
INFLUENCED)
Maintain my facial features (I AM BLACK)
hairstyle (WITH TWO BLACK PARENTS)
and overall likeness (VERY MUCH THICK
NOSED)
but adapt them to fit the distinct (BUT...)
stylized look of anime. (MAKE ME MORE
DIGESTIBLE)

THINK BEFORE CRITIQUE

before you
open that mouth
and spread
hot breath,
your critique
should address
the service
the system
or the structure,
so situate
yourselves
accordingly

WHEW

strengthen your core, chile
failure isn't a lesson
unless
you learn

       stop

              being so
                eager
             to be right

           and be grateful
               to be
                  in
         right relationship

REPRESENTATION IS NOT LIBERATION

you
cannot
c

      oo

         uuu

            nnnn

               ttttt

your way
to freedom

no amount
of tallies
on a sheet
will equal freedom

a ballot box
has never

gotten
me
free

                unless

                          it coincided
               with the economic interests
                  of the power wielders

which means
sometimes

they look like you

but don't have
any interest
in making sure
you
are
                Black
                 and
                alive